by Catherine Podojil

illustrated by Tom McKee

Editorial Offices: Glenview, Illinois • Parsippany, New Jersey • New York, New York
Sales Offices: Needham, Massachusetts • Duluth, Georgia • Glenview, Illinois
Coppell, Texas • Ontario, California • Mesa, Arizona

Molly unwrapped the small package. "A carved giraffe!" she cried excitedly.

She turned on her computer to write an e-mail to her friend Juma.

Dear Juma,
Thank you for the giraffe. It's going to look great on my computer desk!
Molly

Juma lives in East Africa in the country of Tanzania. His father works at a game preserve there.

Molly lives with her dad in Colorado. Her dad is a wildlife biologist.

Molly and Juma met when Molly and her dad visited Tanzania.

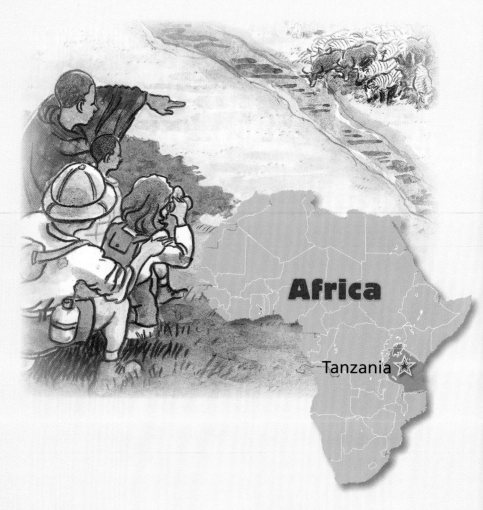

Africa

Tanzania ☆

Dear Molly,
I am glad you like the carving!
Today Father is driving tourists on safari. He is a good tour guide.
Tomorrow I will be playing in a soccer game. Soccer is my favorite sport.
Bye for now,
Juma

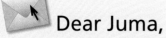 Dear Juma,

I bet you are good at dribbling the soccer ball with your feet. Did your team win the game?

My favorite sports are bike riding and hiking. I like to hike with my dad.

Today is the Fourth of July. It is our biggest holiday! We celebrate our country's independence. Tonight we will watch fireworks. They're very beautiful!
    Until next time,
    Molly

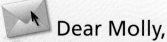 Dear Molly,

Yes, we won! It was a great game!

My other news is that Father found a baby zebra yesterday. She was dangerously far from her herd. Today she wobbled on her tiny legs. Father said she will be more steady each day.

Take care,
Juma

 Dear Juma,

I'd like to see that zebra. During the summer my dad teaches people about wildlife. He is worried about grizzly bears. People are taking over their habitats.

Well, I'm off to do errands.

Molly

Dear Molly,

Yesterday I arranged thirty bundles of food for the animals at the game preserve. I am getting strong for soccer!

Father and I are planning to come to Colorado next year! Do you think we might see grizzly bears there?

Please write soon.

Juma

Dear Juma,

I'm very happy that you are coming to visit! Dad says he will take us up into the mountains to look for grizzly bears!

Your friend and e-pal,

Molly

Tanzania's Wildlife Reserves

Almost one-quarter of Tanzania is now wildlife reserves. The animals in these areas are protected by law. The Selous Game Reserve is the world's largest wildlife park. It is located in southeast Tanzania.

Zebras, wildebeests, and gazelles migrate, or travel, across Tanzania each year. Many lions, elephants, hyenas, black rhinos, and cheetahs live in Tanzania. Tanzania's birds include huge flocks of pink flamingos.